Origin, Symbolism, and Design of the Chartres Labyrinth

Robert Ferré
Director, Labyrinth Enterprises

Illustrations by the author

© 2001 by Robert Ferré
Reprinted 2006

ISBN 0-9779612-1-4

Labyrinth Enterprises
128 Slocum Avenue
St. Louis, MO 63119
(800) 873-9873
www.labyrinth-enterprises.com

ORIGIN, SYMBOLISM, AND DESIGN OF THE CHARTRES LABYRINTH

For some ten years now there has been a revival in the use of labyrinths in the United States and around the world. Churches, in particular, are finding them to be effective tools for prayer, meditation, and turning inward. Many different labyrinth patterns are being used, both traditional and modern. The majority of churches and retreat centers, however, have utilized the pattern found in the nave of Chartres Cathedral in Chartres, France.

Chartres labyrinth.

The purpose of this book is to give the reader a greater depth of understanding about the Chartres labyrinth. As a long-time enthusiast of Chartres (my first visit was in 1965, my 45th and 46th visits in 2001) and as a professional master labyrinth maker, I have gathered together a wide range of information about the origin, symbolism, design, and meaning of this famous labyrinth. This book does not contain instructions on making the Chartres labyrinth. Such details can be found in a companion book, *Constructing the Chartres Labyrinth*, also available from Labyrinth Enterprises.

Although pavement labyrinths originated in Italy, it was in the cathedrals and churches of France that they reached their full flowering. Unless otherwise specified, the towns and churches mentioned in this book are in France.

Manuscript drawings

Many people are surprised to learn that the Chartres pattern did not originate at Chartres. In fact, the path pattern – round, eleven circuits (concentric paths), with cruciform internal turns – had already existed for some 300 years before its installation in Chartres. The design had been developed not as a device for walking, but as an illustration used in manuscripts as far back as the ninth century. Still, the Chartres version was unique in that it established certain proportions for the labyrinth, including size of the center and line/path ratios, as well as adding the petals in the

1

center and the lunations around the perimeter. These features, indeed, were unique to Chartres. Therefore, it is deservedly known as the Chartres labyrinth.

Chartres was in the diocese of Sens, as was the town of Auxerre. It is in the Benedictine monastery of Saint Germain in Auxerre that the oldest extant drawings of the labyrinth may have originated. A crude experimental drawing (illustrated below) was included as part of a manuscript compiled by the monk Heiric of Auxerre around 860. Perhaps he covered the subject of labyrinths in his lectures since we find that his student, Remigius of Auxerre (a famous teacher of the liberal arts), also displayed Chartres-type labyrinths in his manuscripts.

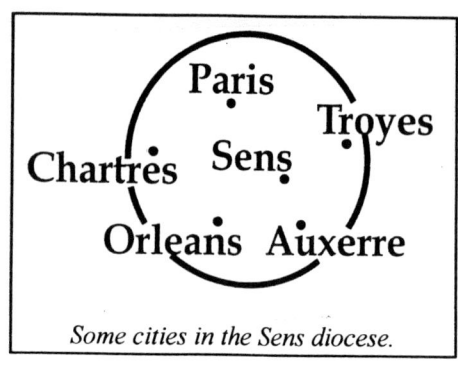

Some cities in the Sens diocese.

At first glance, this drawing isn't very clear. However, while making this illustration, I discovered the scribe's system. At each place where there would eventually be a back-to-back turn (known as a "labrys"), the monk made six marks. Two of them are stylized slashes, which were meant to "open" the circle at that point, in preparation for making a turn. On either side of these slashes, four additional marks indicate that the adjacent circles are meant to be continuous.

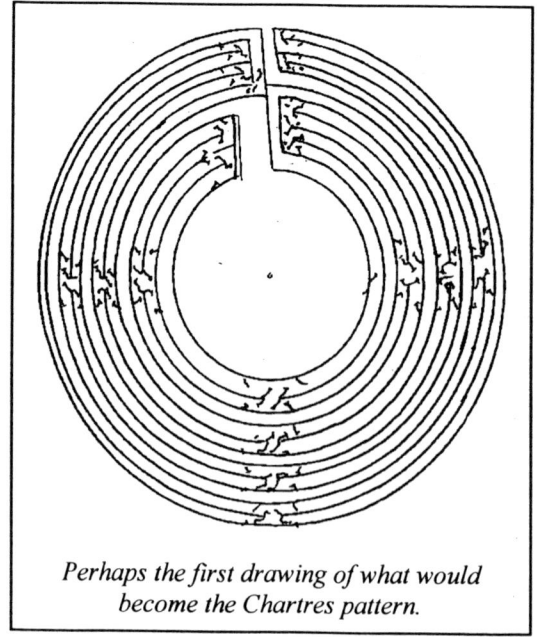

Perhaps the first drawing of what would become the Chartres pattern.

When I myself design new labyrinth patterns, I draw a series of uninterrupted concentric circles on a page. Then, experimenting with placing the turns in different locations, I draw a line for a labrys and put small round circles to indicate where the relevant line stops, opening it for the turn. I suspect that our 9th-century monk friend was experimenting in a similar way. In his manuscript, the page opposite the labyrinth drawing contains a number of circles, apparently a false start in attempting to draw a labyrinth. Nor was the drawing even completed, as the turns were marked but never drawn. Was he inventing the pattern, or just copying it from another source? We may never know.

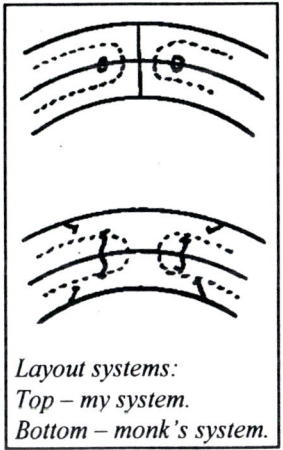

Layout systems:
Top – my system.
Bottom – monk's system.

Drawing the labyrinth, the monk used a compass (shown by a dot in the middle) to get the circles round. Most likely he used a quill compass, a daunting task. Drawings of medieval compasses illustrate a mechanism similar to today's inexpensive compasses made for school children which have a simple arc-shaped sliding mechanism which holds the desired setting in place through friction. Having a tendency to slip, such compasses make it difficult to achieve a high degree of accuracy, as shown by the uneven spacing. Perhaps the monk was not experienced in the use of the compass.

The large center may indicate an original intention to include a drawing in the labyrinth. Usually the entrances of labyrinths are shown facing downward, which in the Middle Ages represented west (not south, as with modern maps). Facing west was indeed the orientation of most medieval church labyrinths, as we shall see.

The Easter connection

Several other manuscripts from Auxerre contained labyrinths. However, Hermann Kern, in his extensive labyrinth compendium entitled *Through the Labyrinth*, considers a different drawing to be the oldest Chartres pattern. It comes from another Saint Germain monastery, Saint-Germain-des-Pres in Paris, similarly dating from the 9th century. This one was drawn freehand rather than using a compass (see illustration on next page). The Saint-Germain-des-Pres labyrinth was included in a work of Easter cycles, calendars, and the like. The Easter connection makes a lot of sense, as we know of Easter dances performed by the clergy on the labyrinths in Auxerre, Sens, and elsewhere (described in detail by Craig Wright and Penelope Reed Doub, see bibliography). Ultimately, the version of the labyrinth built in Chartres included a lunar calendar – the 112 partial circles around the perimeter comprising four lunar months. Hence, these partial circles are sometimes called *lunations*. (French texts tend to call them *dents*, meaning teeth, as the labyrinth looks like a cogged wheel.) The lunar calendar is used for calculating the date of Easter, which occurs on the first Sunday after the first full moon after the spring equinox.

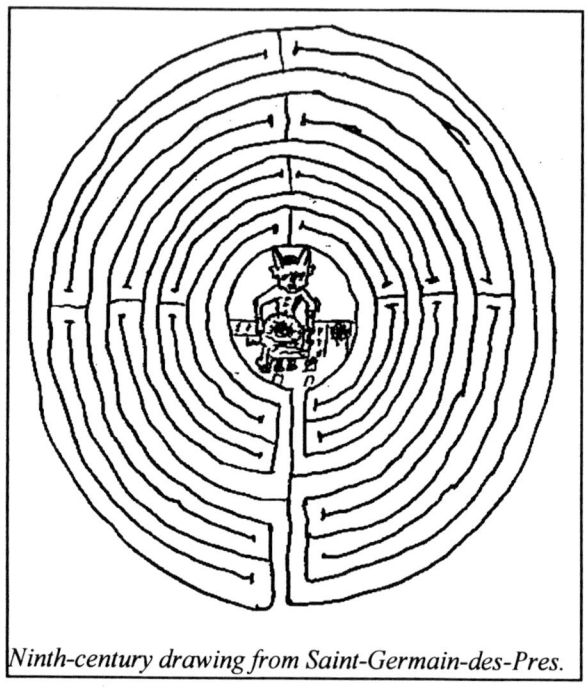

Ninth-century drawing from Saint-Germain-des-Pres.

The text accompanying the above labyrinth quotes Isidore of Seville's definition of a labyrinth. Seville lived in the sixth century, and while some of his manuscripts contain labyrinths, they are generally held to be copies made at later dates. Still, if he was defining labyrinths, they must have been known at his time. The oldest extant church labyrinth, now in Algiers, comes from the Basilica of Reparata in Orleansville, Algeria. It appears to be a typical four-part square Roman labyrinth converted to Christian use by the placement of a design in the center, arranging in rows the letters of the phrase *"Sancta Eclesia"* (holy church). It would be interesting to know if Isidore of Seville himself described Roman labyrinths or some version of the subsequent round Christian design.

4

There are a number of irregularities in the Saint-Germain-des-Pres labyrinth, which may indicate that certain aspects of the pattern weren't yet fixed. For example, in the Chartres labyrinth, the entrance path into the center straddles the vertical axis. Here, however, the line *between* the two entrance paths is on the vertical axis. This would make the entry path into the center offset to the right, not in the middle. To counter this effect, the path leading into the center was made a bit narrower, to give it more of an appearance of being centered, and not to the right.

Note the rather strong marks used to indicate where to open the circles for the turns. This was more efficient than the system used by the Auxerre monk. Most noticeable in this drawing is the devil-like figure in the center, representing the king of this (sinful) world. While not a Minotaur, it certainly reflects the same symbolism.

Theseus and the Minotaur

The Chartres labyrinth originally contained a bronze (or copper) plaque in the center which portrayed the story of Theseus slaying the Minotaur. Yes, a Greek myth was present in the center of the labyrinth in a Gothic cathedral. Although some scholars question what was originally in the center, there are written accounts from eyewitnesses verifying that it was Theseus and the Minotaur. One such account was by Charles Challine, who died in 1678, and another by Vincent Chevard, the mayor of Chartres at the time the plaque was removed in 1792 (along with the bells) to make cannon for the Napoleonic wars.

The Greek myth of Theseus and the Minotaur includes one of the first accounts of a labyrinth, built for King Minos on the island of Crete by Daedalus, the mythical first architect. In French, the word for maze is *dedale*, coming from Daedalus. The labyrinth was built to hold the Minotaur, which had the body of a man but the head of a bull. Theseus succeeded in slaying the monstrous Minotaur, finding his way back out of the maze by following a thread that had been given to him by Ariadne, daughter of King Minos (who in turn, had received it from Daedalus).

Daedalus was considered the inventor of many tools and techniques used by architects. For that reason, he was held in high esteem by medieval masons. The labyrinths in the cathedrals of Amiens and Rheims included figures and/or names of the masons involved in constructing those cathedrals. For that reason, scholars speculate that the labyrinth was a kind of signature, showing the skill of the masons, who were worthy of being associated with the archetypal Daedalus. However, those labyrinths were generations later than the one in Chartres Cathedral. The Amiens labyrinth, for example, was made in 1289, some 88 years after the Chartres labyrinth. It was given the name "House of Daedalus," making the connection to the mythical architect quite clear.

In Chartres, the presence of the Greek myth reflected one of the principles of Scholasticism, the main intellectual orientation of the 12th century. Scholars strove to reframe all of the knowledge passed down from ancient times into a medieval, Christian context – especially the teachings of Pythagorus and Plato. All of history was seen as a precursor to the Christian era. Thus, a story such as Theseus slaying the Minotaur with the aid of a virgin was accepted as a metaphor for salvation through the intercession of the Virgin Mary. It was just one of many so-called "pagan" symbols to be found in Chartres Cathedral.

Most interpreters consider Theseus to represent Christ, the Minotaur to be sin, and the thread to be the teachings or dogma of the church. I myself held this view until speaking recently with Australian architect and Chartres expert John James. Christ wouldn't *need* a thread, he points out, since Christ *is* the thread. It is *we* who need the thread. Hence, Theseus is the pilgrim, the Christian, the seeker, who must overcome his inner fears and temptations (the Minotaur) with the aid of spiritual guidance (the thread).

This interpretation makes much more sense to me. Myths are only superficially about the gods; they are really about us. In her book *Labyrinths: Ancient Paths of Wisdom and Peace,* Virginia Westbury goes into some detail as to possible meanings of the Minotaur myth. She reminds us that Theseus was not a god. A hero, yes, but the whole point of such hero myths is that an "ordinary" person can overcome the trials and tribulations of life – just as all of us must do. The labyrinth can help.

There were precedents for putting the Minotaur in the center of the Chartres labyrinth. In the 12th century, a Chartres-pattern labyrinth was inscribed into the narthex wall at the cathedral of San Martino in Lucca, Italy. Not only did it have a Minotaur in the center, it also included the following inscription:

Here is the labyrinth that Daedalus from Crete built, and which no one can exit once inside; only Theseus was able to do so, thanks to Ariadne's thread.

This inscription may have been reflecting the words of Gregory of Nyssa, one of the church fathers, who commented on the labyrinth way back in the fourth century:

Those who wander, caught in a labyrinth, do not know how to find the way out; but if they meet someone who knows this maze well, they undertake to follow him to the end, through the complicated and misleading turns of the edifice. They would not have escaped had they not followed their guide, step by step. Reflect: The labyrinth of life would be similarly inextricable for man if he did not follow the same path that led Him who once entered back outside.

People may have traced the Lucca labyrinth with their fingers prior to entering into the church – a predecessor of the carved wooden finger labyrinths available today.

The labyrinth as a symbol

The Lucca inscription points out a puzzling and somewhat bizarre circumstance with regards to the history of labyrinths. Throughout history, labyrinths have been used as metaphors for confusion and difficulty, for impossible entry and/or exit. Yet, until the 15th century, all representations of labyrinths were unicursal, which is to say, with a single path that contains no dead ends or false passages. Had Theseus been in a unicursal labyrinth, he wouldn't have needed Ariadne's thread, nor would he have had trouble extricating himself, as this inscription advises.

I believe that such unicursal drawings of the labyrinth were not meant to be taken literally. They represented in a symbolic way the implied, inextricable, multicursal maze. The viewer wasn't supposed to believe that the labyrinth pictured was the exact one that entrapped the Minotaur. In actual practice, a unicursal labyrinth leads unerringly to the center. As a symbol, however, the labyrinth *represents* our confused and errant path through this world, which in no way assumes success. In a maze, some people never reach the center, while others succeed as a fluke. Such a concept would be far too difficult to portray literally.

Instead, the nature of a maze is represented simply, metaphorically. In the case of the classical 7-circuit labyrinth, which was once stamped into coins from Crete, it is a pattern that we can draw fairly easily, but which still looks somewhat complex. Performing rituals on the labyrinth would not be possible using an actual maze, with participants wandering around

7

aimlessly, lost, perplexed, unable to perform their part in the ceremony. Actual chaos would result, whereas the purpose of the labyrinth is only to *seem* chaotic, to stylize chaos. If using a maze for ceremony, it would be necessary in advance to let everyone in on the secret, so they knew the right path to take. Easier still would be to draw *only* the correct path, and omit the dead ends completely. As such, the labyrinth represents the *solution* to the maze, victory over difficulty and hardship.

And so, it seems that the hero myth, of which the Minotaur was only one in a long series dating back millennia, was articulated yet again, this time in a Christian context. Another example of such use was found in a manuscript that was most likely written in Auxerre and later found at the nearby Cistercian monastery of Pontigny. Along with a Chartres-type labyrinth the text gave an account and discussion of the myth of Theseus and the Minotaur. Previously, antiquity had adopted the classical 7-circuit labyrinth as the symbol for the Greek myth. In Christian times, the Chartres labyrinth pattern was used for the assimilation of this archetypal story in a new context.

Italian pavement labyrinths

While manuscript labyrinths may have originated in France, the first actual pavement labyrinths are found in Italy. Perhaps the earliest such labyrinth

of the Chartres type was installed around 1150 in the basilica of San Michele Maggiore in Pavia, Italy. Part of the labyrinth was covered by the altar. Ultimately, only the covered portion survived. We know the larger design, however, from a rather crude 17th-century drawing, which I have redrawn in the illustration to the left, omitting some printing in the center.

8

The artist confused Centaur with Minotaur, drawing the body of a bull and the head and shoulders of a man, whereas the Minotaur is just the opposite. This particular Centaur has just decapitated a victim and is holding its head as Theseus sneaks up behind him to club him. Here we have a very graphic example of evil in operation in the world, which each of us must overcome.

For some reason, the center drawing is not oriented toward the entrance to the labyrinth (nor are the exterior images in the same orientation as the center). Even more confusing is the location of the altar, which covered that portion of the labyrinth above the horizontal line.

Note how simple and cartoon-like the drawing is. Such was the case not only for manuscript drawings but also for early stained glass windows, such as those found in Chartres. Figures are portrayed with large heads and simple features. Again, it was the story which was important, not the drawing itself. As with the labyrinth representing a maze, the image itself wasn't meant to be taken literally. Later, not long after Chartres Cathedral was built, shading, perspective, and realistic figures became the accepted style. At that point, the medium and the message became more confused – the imagination was thwarted as we were told (through realism) exactly the way things "ought" to look (literally).

Origin of the path pattern

There was an identifiable process in the development and creation of a Christian labyrinth, which was derived from the older, 7-circuit classical labyrinth. First the labyrinth was made round. Then the number of paths was increased to 11, a number associated with sin, excess, and depravity. From this, we can deduce that the labyrinth was clearly intended to symbolize our earthly experience. The same conclusion can be reached given the location of the labyrinth in the nave of Chartres Cathedral, a counterpoint to the altar at the other end of the cathedral.

A different 11-circuit path pattern was created by Otfrid, a 9th-century monk in Germany. He started with the classical 7-circuit, made it round, and then added more circuits to the outside to arrive at 11. Eventually, the Chartres path pattern was discovered and the labryses were added to give it a cruciform appearance. How the Chartres pattern evolved can be demonstrated more clearly by looking at the seed patterns.

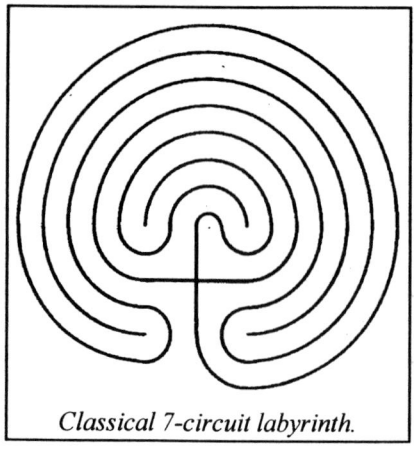
Classical 7-circuit labyrinth.

Round classical 7-circuit.

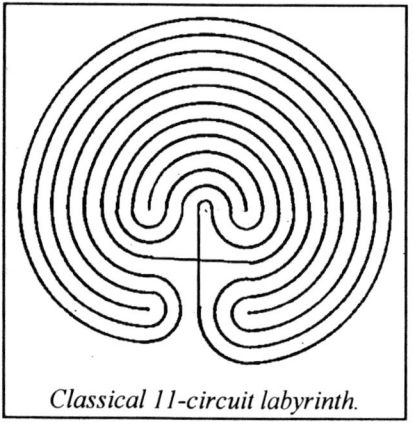
Classical 11-circuit labyrinth.

Here are the various labyrinth patterns which preceded the Chartres pattern.

Classical 11-circuit made round.

Otfrid 11-circuit round pattern.

Seed patterns

The labyrinths that we are examining are essentially round except for the entrance, which is formed of straight lines. The turns arranged on either side of the entrance determine the path pattern. Therefore, the entrance configuration is called the seed pattern. By connecting the elements of the seed pattern, one necessarily arrives at the design of the labyrinth. The seed pattern of the 7-circuit labyrinth has been known for a long time. For example, a church in Scandinavia has a classical 7-circuit labyrinth painted blue – but the seed pattern is painted red, thereby showing how it was made.

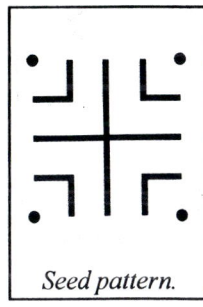
Seed pattern.

To form the seed pattern for the classical 7-circuit labyrinth, make an equal-armed cross with a bracket and a dot in each quadrant. To draw the labyrinth, start at the top of the cross and make a half-circle connecting it to the top of the bracket on the right of the cross. Next, connect the top of the bracket on the left to the next available element on the right, which is the dot. Continue to connect the next available elements on each side of the labyrinth. The final line will be from the bottom bracket on the left all the way around to the bottom of the cross.

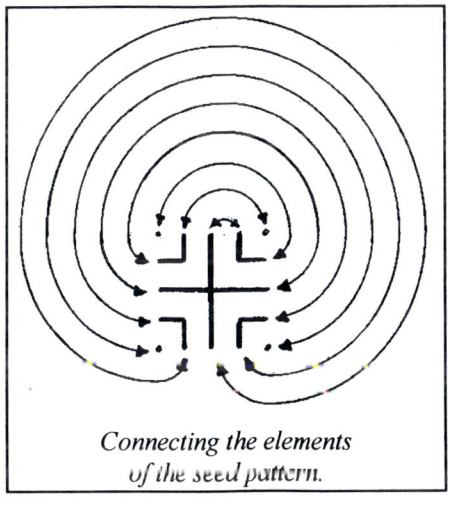
Connecting the elements of the seed pattern.

When finished, note that the cross is to the left of the center of the labyrinth, and that the first turn is also to the left. This is called a left-handed labyrinth. The Chartres labyrinth is left-handed, since the first turn after entering the labyrinth is to the left. To make a right-handed labyrinth from the seed pattern above, make the first half-circle from the top of the cross to the bracket on the left. That half-circle forms the center of the labyrinth. Since it is to the left of the cross, the cross is therefore to the right of the center, thereby assuring a right-handed labyrinth in which the first turn will be to the right.

11

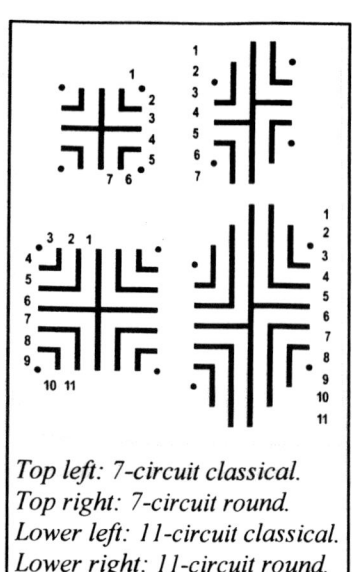

Top left: 7-circuit classical.
Top right: 7-circuit round.
Lower left: 11-circuit classical.
Lower right: 11-circuit round.

The classical 11-circuit labyrinth is constructed by adding another bracket in each quadrant so that there are two brackets and one dot. I call these "nested" brackets. The classical labyrinth is not symmetrical, having one more circuit on one side than the other. To make this design circular, the two sides must be symmetrical. This is accomplished by changing the seed pattern so that the arms of the cross are offset. The same arm as the handedness, in this case the left arm, is shifted to be one circuit lower than the opposing arm. Essentially, the cross is lost. This change, however, still isn't enough to make the labyrinth circular, as the seed pattern is too condensed to connect the various elements. It must be stretched out by elongating the brackets. Note the comparison of the various seed patterns. At the top, the 7-circuit pattern is shown in both of its configurations. The corresponding seed patterns for the 11-circuit are shown underneath.

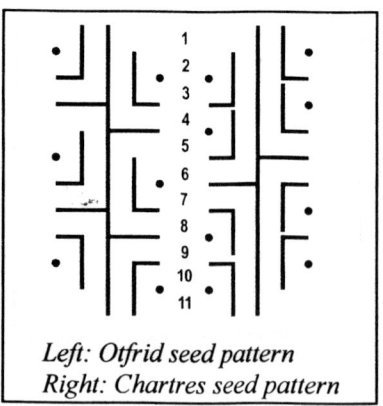

Left: Otfrid seed pattern
Right: Chartres seed pattern

Now, look at the seed patterns for the Chartres and the Otfrid patterns (left illustration). Both are 11-circuit labyrinths, but the seed patterns are narrower and more efficient. This was accomplished by stacking rather than nesting the brackets. In the case of the Otfrid pattern, the cross has two arms on each side, and only three brackets, whereas the Chartres labyrinth has four brackets and a cross with two offset arms, like the classical 11-circuit labyrinth.

Why wasn't the Chartres pattern made with classical nested brackets? If you add the labryses you will find that the nested pattern doesn't work. It leaves unreachable isolated islands. But the stacked brackets do work. All of this discussion about seed patterns, nesting and stacking was to reach the following conclusion as to how the Chartres pattern evolved. It borrowed

12

from both the classical and the Otfrid patterns. As with the classical, there are two brackets in each quadrant of the cross. At the same time, the Chartres pattern has stacked brackets, as with the Otfrid pattern, rather than nesting them. While it is easy to point out this small variation, it took several centuries for it to actually be developed. The analysis of the seed patterns also shows how closely the Chartres pattern is related to the classical pattern, even though they look completely different. Truly, they are at least cousins, if not sisters.

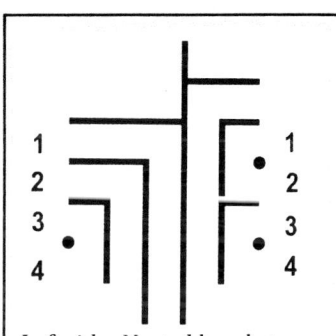

Left side: Nested brackets.
Right side: Stacked brackets.
Each type creates four paths.

The labyrinth pattern involves a principle found in nature known as close packing. Its circular shape and circuitous paths attain the longest possible distance within a small amount of space. The brain and intestines use close packing, which is why their convolutions resemble labyrinths. In the Chartres labyrinth, a rule of thumb is that the length of the path is equal to approximately 20 times the diameter. That means a diameter of 42 feet produces a path length of approximately 840 feet. (To be precise, it is 850 feet.) A round trip, therefore, equals one-third of a mile.

Now that you know what to look for, note the seed pattern within the Chartres labyrinth. (Lines end at dots in the seed pattern.)

I am often asked about making a Chartres labyrinth that is wheelchair accessible. If I were to make the paths three feet wide, the lines would be eight inches wide and the whole labyrinth would be 104 feet in diameter. Multiplying by 20, that gives a path length of 2,080 feet, with the round trip being twice that, or more than three-fourths of a mile. That is likely too long

13

for most people to cover in a wheelchair. The solution is to make the entire labyrinth a hard surface, such as concrete or brick pavers, with paths a more normal size. Wheelchairs can simply straddle the path with the wheels in the adjacent paths. Thus it is possible to have an accessible labyrinth of manageable length.

Sacred geometry

In the Middle Ages, Chartres was the home of a famous cathedral school that was a leading center of Platonism. The curriculum was based on the seven liberal arts, including geometry. Today, in the 21st century, the words "sacred geometry" seem to be an oxymoron. We see mathematics as a cold, computer-like discipline unrelated to anything remotely sacred. In former times, however, especially from Pythagorus (died 497 B.C.E.) and Plato (died 347 B.C.E.) through the Middle Ages, geometry was akin to philosophy and even theology. Its purpose was to understand and imitate God's act of Creation. Geometry was sacred precisely because it comprised the rules and lawfulness that God established to create the physical world.

Sacred geometry was an attempt to reverse the process of Creation through studying nature and the cosmos, reducing it to its most basic elements of geometry, thereby understanding what God had done. The school at Chartres studied Plato's *Timaeus* because of its detailed cosmology. Over the centuries, certain numbers and proportions came to hold specific Christian significance. By incorporating them in the cathedral and the labyrinth, these places came to express a kind of universal language and symbolism. To point these out, I must first give a brief summary of sacred geometry.

The principles of sacred geometry in the Middle Ages came through the interpretations of Nicomachus, Macrobius, St. Augustine, and Boethius. Important medieval writers included Hugh of St. Victor and Thierry of Chartres. It is hard to overestimate the importance of numbers, their characteristics, and their interactions. The modern equivalent would be the adjective "scientific." Modern society gives great credibility and belief to anything that is considered scientific. Science offers a paradigm to manage the complexity of the universe and give it order. In the Middle Ages, several centuries prior to the evolution of modern science, numbers were given the same importance. The relationships and properties of numbers were used to explain everything in the world, visible and invisible. After all, numbers were the building blocks that God used for the Creation, and were thus imbued with sacred meaning.

14

These days, we think of atoms as the building blocks of the material world, but atoms themselves are composed of both number and shape (geometry). Consider this comment by the 2nd-century Greek writer Nicomachus of Gerasa from his book, *Introduction to Arithmetic*:

All that has by nature with systematic method been arranged in the universe seems both in part and as a whole to have been determined and ordered in accordance with number; by the forethought and the mind of Him that created all things; for the pattern was fixed, like a preliminary sketch, by the domination of number pre-existent in the mind of the world-creating God . . . .

Geometers studied nature, which makes sense, as the word itself means "measuring the earth." In the process, the *qualities* of certain numbers became apparent. In our age of computers and calculators, numbers are generally just considered for their *quantitative* aspects. Whether counting apples on the shelf or atoms in the universe, this is still a narrow use and understanding of numbers.

In earlier times, mathematicians were also philosophers, because numbers and proportions present a timeless, universal, and precise language for expressing metaphysical truths. Each number has a specific meaning. *One* is not considered to be a number so much as a principle – the monad from which all other numbers originate. *Two* reflects duality, opposites, the division (not addition) of *one*. *Three*, in Christian terms, is associated with the Trinity, and therefore the soul and the spiritual. *Four* stands for the material world, the four directions, the four corners of the earth, the four elements of fire, earth, air and water.

Throughout history the greatest attention has been paid to the numbers *three* and *four*. By combining these numbers, we fully integrate the physical and spiritual, becoming complete beings. This is our goal here on earth. These numbers can be combined by addition, which gives *seven*, or by multiplication, which yields *twelve*. Seven and twelve, by far the most mystical and mysterious of all numbers, are found throughout Chartres Cathedral and the labyrinth.

It takes twelve concentric circles to make an 11-circuit labyrinth. *Voila*, the number 12. But while twelve is a particularly revered number, eleven has less than happy associations. Twelve is the number of enlightenment, whereas 11 represents obfuscation and confusion, excess and inadequacy. Thus the labyrinth embraces both success and failure, integration and isolation. Just as God created the world yet the world is filled with sin and depravity, the number 12 creates the labyrinth, yet 11 paths imply our shortcomings. The opposite is also true. However hopeless and terrible the mundane, physical world may seem, it is literally surrounded by spiritual enlightenment. The presence of twelve holds the promise of the integration of our two natures, physical and spiritual. In this way, the labyrinth accurately reflects the elements and possibilities of our common pilgrimage.

Sacred geometry led to another enterprise known as numerology. Numerology is to sacred geometry what astrology is to astronomy. In this regard, the terrorist attacks in the United States on September 11, 2001, have many associations with the number 11, not the least of which is the huge 11 made by the towers themselves. That day was the 254th day of the year, the digits of which add up to 11. Remaining in the year, therefore, were 111 days. Flight number 11 hit one of the towers, and the number of passengers on two planes (65 and 92) add up to 11 – as do the number of letters in New York City and The Pentagon. Of course some of this may just be coincidence (after all, my name, Robert Ferré, has 11 letters). In noting these associations, it can be like discovering the pattern for eyes on potatoes (yes, there is one) or the 10-part division of all squashes. You begin to realize that there may be a plan behind Creation. Geometry!

Lines have width

With this basic knowledge of sacred geometry, we can now discover the presence of these numbers within the labyrinth and its setting. By knowing some of this language, we can read the message that medieval masons left for us to decipher. First, let's look at the lines.

In 1995 I spend several months in the midst of a very mystical experience, studying the geometry of the Chartres labyrinth. One of the discoveries that opened up its secrets to me was the fact that *lines have width*. This occurred to me as I tried to imagine myself as the mason whose job it was to cut the blue-black marble out of which the lines of the labyrinth were made. The instructions wouldn't have been sufficient to simply say, "Make a line." As a mason, I would have had to know how *wide* the line needed to be.

When we see a drawing of the labyrinth in a book, in such small scale the lines are just single lines. But in reality, the lines of the Chartres labyrinth are three inches wide. Proportionally, the ratio of line to path is 2:9. Think of the entire line/path entity as having 11 units (the same as the number of

16

circuits). Two of the units are line and nine are path. As such, the line is proportionally wider than most people draw it.

For the circular lines, therefore, there are two different diameters, one to the inside of the line, towards the center of the labyrinth, and the other to the outside of the line. How then do we measure the diameter of a circle? We could measure to the inside, to the outside, or split the difference and measure to the center of the line. The answer is, "All of the above." By using these different measurements, the masons who built the labyrinth were able to incorporate different proportions, and therefore layers of meaning, depending on which measurement (and numbers) they used. Hence, in my discussion of proportions, I will specify to which *part* of the line (inside, outside, or center) the measurements or ratios pertain.

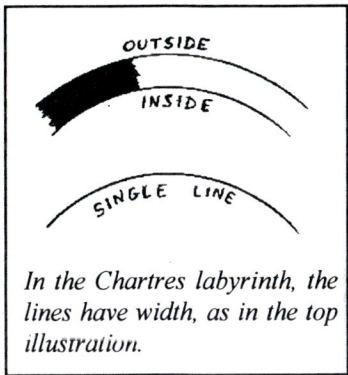

In the Chartres labyrinth, the lines have width, as in the top illustration.

Proportions of the center

One of the important contributions of the Chartres labyrinth was to establish certain proportions, including the size of the center. The diagram below indicates several such proportions.

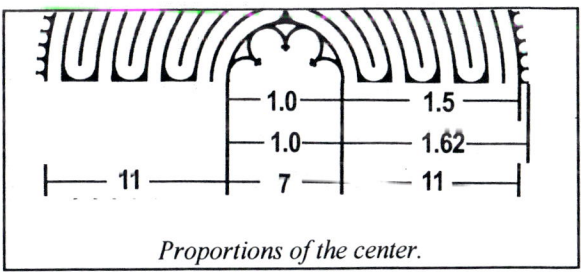

Proportions of the center.

To find the overall proportion of the center, we measure the inner and outer circles (not including the lunations), measuring to their outside diameters. We find that the center is one-fourth the diameter of the labyrinth. Here, then, is the number four, representing this world, and more specifically, our path or journey through this world. At the same time, the ratio of the center to the rest of the labyrinth is 1:3. This is an expression of fourths, with the

17

center being *one*-fourth and the rest of the labyrinth being *three*-fourths, hence 1:3. This ratio introduces the important number three, which pertains to the labyrinth on *both* sides of the center. To calculate the ratio of the center circle to *one* side of the labyrinth, we divide three in half, giving us the ratio of 1:1.5, as shown on the drawing.

When examining the lunations, I was certain that they would be formed using a geometric shape of great importance, called the *vesica piscis*. Also known as the *mandorla*, this shape encompasses the overlapping area of two circles of the same size, each with their center on the perimeter of the other. The two circles again represent our two natures, human and divine. The *vesica* is the integration of those two natures, similar to the joining of the numbers three and four. On the front of many Romanesque churches (as well as Chartres Cathedral, which has a Romanesque facade), Jesus is portrayed in the center of a *vesica*, since He represents both circles, God and man, the ultimate integration of both natures.

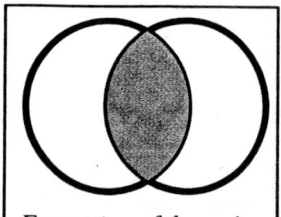

Formation of the vesica piscis, *the space shared by both circles.*

The portion of the circle remaining outside of the *vesica* can be measured in two ways: three-fourths of the diameter (note: three and four) or two-thirds of the circumference. These exact measurements are reflected in the petal circles, and so I thought the same would be true for the lunations. But when I measured the lunations, I found that the diameters were a little too short to have been determined by a *vesica*. I was puzzled by the loss of such great symbolism, until I discovered a different proportion, pertaining to the size of the center. The two elements of the ratio include the diameter of the center (measured to the center of the line) – to which we assign the value 1.0 – and the distance from that point to the tip of the lunation, which results in a relative value of 1.62. This ratio, 1:1.62, is known as the golden mean.

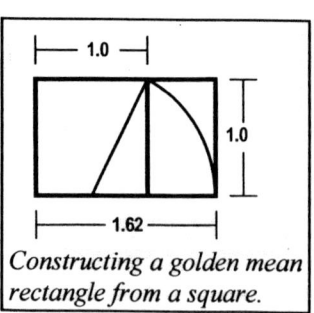

Constructing a golden mean rectangle from a square.

The golden mean is a very sacred measurement as it reflects the growth pattern in nature. A rectangle with the dimensions of the golden mean ratio has been shown to be the most pleasing shape to the eye, and thus has been incorporated widely in art and architecture – from

18

cathedrals to the United Nations building in New York. You will notice that the center of the Chartres labyrinth is larger than most previous versions, which tended to have small centers. It reflects these important measurements: the fraction 1/4, the ratios 1:3 and 1:1.5, and the golden mean, with its ratio of 1:1.62. But there's even more to notice about the center with respect to another mystical mathematical value.

Measured to the center of the line, the center circle of the labyrinth closely approximates seven line/path units. There are 11 such units on either side of the center, for a total of 22. Thus, in addition to the previous 1:3 ratio we can also find a 7:22 ratio. In the Middle Ages, the fraction 22/7 was commonly used for the value of *pi*, the relationship between the diameter and the circumference of a circle. The modern equivalent for *pi* is 3.1416, whereas 22/7 equals 3.1429, a very small error of only four hundredths of one percent.

Incidentally, the horizontal lintel stones at Stonehenge, in England, were constructed to reflect the same ratio. If you take the width of the stones as the diameter of a circle, the length proves to be the circumference of that same circle. The value of *pi* is a transcendent number, which can't be calculated definitively. As a decimal, it goes on forever, with no repeated patterns. But it can be drawn and expressed precisely through geometry.

The labryses

The back-to-back turns in the labyrinth are called labryses because they look like the mythical double-headed ax carried by Amazon women warriors and used for decoration in the palace at Knossos in Crete – location of the Minotaur myth. Some people think that the word labyrinth derives from the word labrys, but most scholars disagree. The similarity, however, sometimes leads to labrys being misspelled l-a-b-y-r-s and pronounced "lab-ears." Actually, the "r" comes before the "y" and it is pronounced "lab-ris."

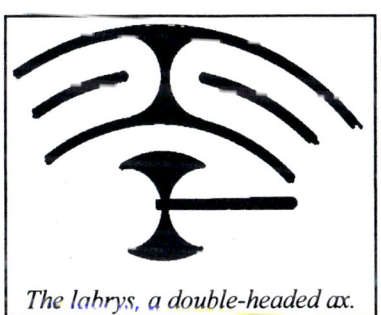
The labrys, a double-headed ax.

There are ten labryses in the Chartres pattern, one for each circle except for the inner and outer circles. Each circle is opened to make room for the back-to-back turns. Counting from the center outward, the first labrys is on the vertical axis, on circle 2. The

19

second labrys is on the right horizontal axis, on circle 3. The third labrys is on the left horizontal axis, on circle 4. And so it continues, with the fourth labrys at the top, the fifth labrys on the right, and so forth. The labryses, if connected by curved arcs, form an outward clockwise spiral.

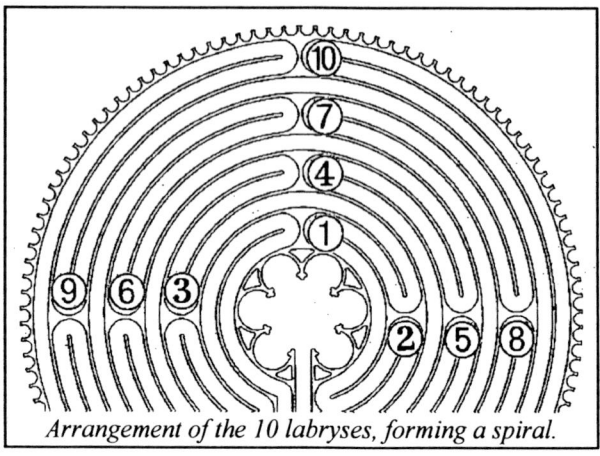
Arrangement of the 10 labryses, forming a spiral.

It is the labryses that give the labyrinth its cruciform shape, an important step in the Christianization of the labyrinth pattern. It is not unique in that respect, however. The alchemical symbol for earth is a circle with a cross in it, just like the labyrinth. Another popular medieval symbol was the wheel of fortune, round with spokes – not dissimilar to the labyrinth and also representing our path through life. Native American medicine wheels also hold a certain resemblance to the labyrinth.

The cruciform shape creates additional numerical symbolism. Note that there are four labryses along the top vertical axis and four half-labryses along the bottom vertical axis on either side of the entrance paths. Hence, the vertical axes have four turns, whereas the horizontal axes each have three turns. As a result, there are seven 180-degree turns in each quadrant of the labyrinth. There's that number seven again. The total number of 180-degree turns for the labyrinth is therefore 28, the same number of days in a lunar month. To these, add the six 90-degree turns along the entrance paths for a total number of 34 turns (three and four!). Other labyrinth patterns with different labrys arrangements don't achieve such consistent and important numerical significance.

The importance of the cruciform shape and the number four is shown by one of the earliest representations of the labyrinth in a manuscript by Spanish scholar Isidore of Seville (died 636), copied in the 11th century. In

This Isidore of Seville manuscript drawing is very Chartres-like except for the entrance.

Located beside the labyrinth, this figure emphasizes the division into four quadrants.

fact, that drawing is the only one among the manuscript drawings that makes the labryses rounded. All of the others just used a straight line. For this reason, Hermann Kern believes that this labyrinth was the one which actually inspired the Chartres labyrinth. Personally, I doubt that. Accompanying the labyrinth was a second drawing which had only two circles and an equal armed cross which divides them into four quadrants. The Latin inscriptions (which I didn't reproduce) advise us to spurn the world (*"spernere mundum"*). Here the division of the circle into four by the labryses clearly invokes the physical world.

Earth measurements

Ancient peoples knew the circle and the cross as the horizon and the four cardinal directions. Research shows that megalithic circles and standing stone formations reflect knowledge of the solar system and the size of the earth. Primitive doesn't mean ignorant. No ancient people destroyed the ozone layer and then refused to do anything to correct it because it might cost jobs. Our forebears knew about the turning of the night sky, the cycle of the seasons, the abundance of the earth. The reported medieval belief that the world was flat is exaggerated. The Greeks estimated quite accurately the size of the earth. The builders of Stonehenge used lengths of measure that relate to the polar diameter of the earth. Should we be surprised, then, at the following mind-boggling statistic? *The diameter of the Chartres labyrinth is one-millionth the diameter of the earth.*

There are three diameters for the labyrinth: To the outside of the 12th circle, to the center of the lunation circles, and to the tips of the lunations. The diameter to the center of the lunations equals 12,720 millimeters. The diameter of the earth is 12,746 kilometers. The difference between the two numbers is 26 out of 12,746 for a minuscule error of two-tenths of one percent. Since the diameter of the labyrinth is also one-tenth the length of the cathedral, the cathedral itself also relates to the size of the earth. Again, geometry is based on earth measure.

The petals

The six petals derive from a basic exercise of geometry. They do not, by the way, reflect the geometry of a "hidden" thirteen-pointed star, an erroneous theory proposed by Keith Critchlow in 1972 and repeated in a number of labyrinth books. I have studied with Keith, and he admits that his theory "doesn't measure out," but he likes the symbolism (12 disciples plus Christ = 13). In fact, the meaning of the petals relates not to the disciples but to Mary, to whom the cathedral is dedicated.

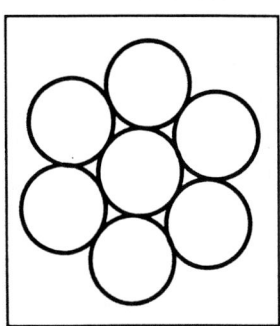

One of the most elementary geometrical designs is one circle surrounded by six others, all exactly the same size, all just touching each other. Anyone practicing drawing with a compass soon discovers this relationship. Stated in another way, the radius of any circle can be used to divide its circumference into six equal divisions. For that reason, six is second only to eight as a basis for the geometric pattern of rose windows.

Seven, then, is the relevant number with regards to the petal design, even though we only see six petals. Seven, it seems, is the only number in the first ten numbers (1-10) that neither generates nor is generated by another number via multiplication. Five is not generated by any other number, but five times two generates 10. Seven stands alone – it neither begets nor is begotten. For that reason, it has been known since ancient times as "the virgin." Seven is the number of virginity. Chartres Cathedral is dedicated to the Virgin Mary because of the great hope that she could act as intercessor and help one attain Paradise. The center of the labyrinth represents Heaven, the goal of our earthly journey. The chance of arriving there is enhanced by Mary's help and by her status. It makes sense that the geometry of the petals, therefore, is based on the number of the Virgin.

The diameters of the petal circles are exactly one-third the diameter of the center of the labyrinth, showing the exact relationship of the seven-circle diagram. Space for the entrance is not created by making the petal circles smaller (as with the 13-pointed star), but by simply overlapping them slightly. The first diagram to the left shows the circles drawn individually, as if they were, say, three inches wide. That's not how the petals look. They look like the second diagram, in which the circles are overlapped, sharing one line between them. So doing, they open space for the entrance path without reducing their size. Since they overlap five times, that means the path should be equal to five line widths, right? Wrong. That would be too easy. It actually equals 4.5 line widths, reflecting the line/path ratio of 2:9 (which is the same as 1:4.5).

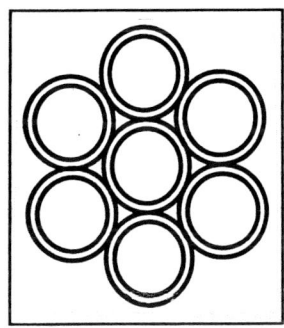

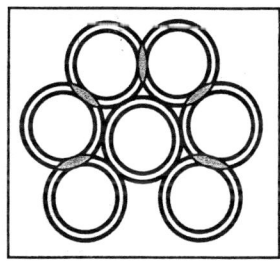

A number of different meanings have been assigned to the six petals. That's one of the benefits of a labyrinth – it lends itself to many different applications. The petals can correspond to six realms, for example, being mineral, vegetable, animal, human, angelic, and divine. Historically, there is no record from the 13th century that suggests what the petals indicate. The rose, of course, was a sign for Mary. We might also consider that the number six is a very perfect number. In fact it is unique because its factors, 1, 2, and 3, can arrive at the number six either through multiplication *or* addition. So, we could see our journey through the labyrinth as moving ever closer to perfection

Christ is in the center, in the form of the crosses at the terminus of the petals (not to mention the cruciform shape of the labyrinth as a whole). There is yet another connection to Christ, this one pertaining to Creation. Although the Creation story is about God, it's hard to portray God. So medieval representations of Creation showed Jesus, holding a compass, working on a globe. I mention this because Creation was accomplished in six days, and there are six petals. For geometers who are imitating the act of Creation, this could not have been a coincidence. Once again, through the design, they succeeded in incorporating several meanings, including the numbers six and seven.

Jesus and Mary are represented throughout the cathedral and the labyrinth, of course. Their relationship is also implied within the sun and moon imagery, since the sun's glory is reflected in the moon as Jesus' glory is reflected in Mary.

The lunations

We have already mentioned that the lunations form a four-month lunar calendar, and that the length of the teeth is determined by a golden mean ratio. Were there no entrance, there would be 114 lunations. One is missing for the entrance, however, comprised of a tooth and half a circle on either side of it. That leaves 113 lunations. However, one of the circles is divided by the entrance path, leaving 112 whole lunation circles. Four 28-day lunar months total 112 days.

The Koran, the scripture for the religion of Islam, has 114 books, but the first one is not counted as such, as it is known as "the entry." Hm-m-m-m, 113 plus an entry, just like the lunations in the labyrinth. At the time the labyrinth was being built knowledge was flooding into Europe from the Arabic world, which was highly sophisticated and erudite compared to barbarian Europe. Moorish Spain was a major site of information exchange. Indeed, in the 12th century, the influential Benedictine abbey in Cluny, France, had the Koran translated into Latin. The rose windows found in cathedrals resemble the geometry of Muslim "stars" too closely for there to be no connection.

Keith Critchlow, whose theory of the 13-pointed star is rather errant, also proposed that the rose window in Chartres, if hinged, would fall exactly on the labyrinth. However, in actuality, the centers would miss hitting each other by more than five feet. Hardly an exact hit. Yet, there is a relationship. According to the immensely detailed study of Chartres Cathedral by Australian architect John James, it was the same mason who laid out the cathedral after the fire of 1194 who also made the labyrinth in 1201. He then left, returning fifteen years later to make the western rose window. Do the meanings relate to each other? Well, the labyrinth represents our journey through this life. The rose window, on the other hand, portrays the Last Judgment – the end result of our journey.

As we saw earlier, the petals in the center of the labyrinth relate to the Virgin Mary. While the labyrinth clearly reflects moon symbolism, so does Mary herself. Like the moon, she is the reflection of the sun/Son. Throughout the cathedral, representations of the sun and moon abound. For example, using the foot measure with which the cathedral was originally laid out, the total length of the cathedral turns out to be an interesting number: 365 and 1/4 feet. Yes, a solar year. So the entire cathedral is solar, reflecting the light of Christ, and His reflection is seen in the moon/Mary/labyrinth. Incidentally, the two towers of Chartres Cathedral are distinctive because of their varying styles (one Romanesque, the other Baroque) and their different heights. On top of the north tower, the taller of the two, is a weathervane featuring the sun. The south tower (which, notably, is 28 feet shorter), has a weathervane of the moon.

Location of the labyrinth

I consider the best estimate for the construction date of the labyrinth to be 1201. For that reason, in August of 2001 I went to Chartres with a group of people to celebrate the labyrinth's 800th birthday. As they are wont to do, scholars disagree on that date. However, I believe John James' work is the most credible. He studied Chartres Cathedral stone by stone for six years. His work has now expanded to include 1500 extant Gothic structures in the Paris Basin.

James' system for dating is based on physical evidence, which he identifies in the stonework itself. He has come to know many of the masons by their personal style, their templates, their geometric constructions, the width of the coursing, and other traits. His work leads us to the subject of mortar. The mortar used in the Middle Ages wasn't the same as modern mortar. These days, Portland cement hardens by hydration. When you add water, it changes the chemical structure (specifically, the calcium silicates C_3S and C_2S form the compounds calcium hydroxide and calcium silicate hydrate), which in turn leads to rapid hardening.

A different type of mortar was used in medieval times. It was kept soft by burning the lime to remove the oxygen and then storing the mortar as a slurry in a hole in the ground until it was used. It hardened by re-absorbing oxygen, which took months. After, say, ten courses of stone had been laid in a wall, any additional weight would squeeze out the still-wet mortar if further height were attempted. So workers had to stop work and wait for a number of months for the mortar to dry before continuing. In a large project, they sometimes went to another portion of the building. Often, however, the masons packed up and left for other jobs. A few months later, a different team of masons would be engaged to continue the work. This system of multiple campaigns led to identifiable changes in style which help to date the structure and determine the chronology of its construction.

Given the importance of Chartres Cathedral and the considerable amount of money raised for its reconstruction, one could assume that the most talented mason of his time would have been given the task of designing the layout for the new cathedral. Indeed, James' work shows that that mason was the same person who made the labyrinth and the rose window. One can conclude, therefore, that the labyrinth was not an afterthought but an integral part of the master mason's design from the very beginning.

Craig Wright, in his book *The Maze and the Warrior*, inexplicably assigns the date of 1215 to the labyrinth, making the following comment (he uses the words maze and labyrinth interchangeably):

The maze is not fundamental to the structure of the church; it is ornamental. ... It did not influence, but merely gave added meaning to, the master plan of the building wrought a priori *by means of geometry. Never, for example, did the size or location of the labyrinth determine the width of the central vessel or the position of the pillars that support it. ... Like the steeple atop the central crossing, the maze was an optional element of architectural design added* a posteriori *to the completed sanctuary.*

I disagree wholeheartedly. Frankly, I don't think that Wright studied the cathedral in enough detail to come to such a conclusion. For one, Chartres doesn't have a steeple above the central crossing. So he must have been speaking about churches in general. Clearly Wright didn't notice the seven bays of the nave. There are four equal bays (arches that lead from the nave into the side aisles) between the center of the labyrinth and the crossing, just as there are four between the crossing and the altar. Hence, the labyrinth and the altar are equidistant from the center of the cathedral. In the nave, however, there are three more bays, extending from the center of the labyrinth to the towers. (We're getting familiar now with these numbers: seven bays, divided by the labyrinth into four and three.) The remaining distance from the fourth bay to the towers was fixed, as the towers were already in place. To fit three bays into the remaining space, each bay gets increasingly smaller. In fact, the seventh bay, next to the tower, becomes so

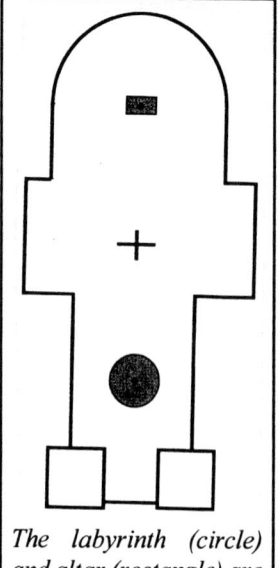

The labyrinth (circle) and altar (rectangle) are equidistant from the center of the crossing.

narrow that there are only three arcades in the triforium level instead of the usual four, as with the other bays.

If the labyrinth were an afterthought, as Wright suggests, then the seven bays of the nave would have been constructed of equal size, as in other cathedrals. But they weren't. In fact, a prodigious effort was made to locate the center of the labyrinth where it is, which *did* involve influencing the placement of pillars, and which *must* have been part of the original plan since the eastern and western ends of the cathedral were constructed simultaneously. The diminishing size of the nave bays is visible in this photograph in which the bays are numbered. The fourth bay, on the right, is the same size as bays 1-3, and as the four bays in the choir. Bay five, however, is noticeably smaller, and bay six even more so. Bay seven is hard to see, but it is smaller yet.

North side of nave: Bay 4 is normal size, 5 is narrower, 6 narrower still, 7 is downright squashed (buttress is at the white line).

Did the labyrinth determine the "width of the central vessel"? I have located in the layout of the cathedral the presence of a progression of root squares. These involve proportions pertaining to the square roots of two, three, and five – all of which are transcendent and therefore mystical numbers. These roots do, in fact, determine the width of the vessel. How is the labyrinth involved? All of these values derive from a beginning base measurement. That base value is the distance from the center of the labyrinth to the center of the crossing.

The crossing in Chartres is rectangular, whereas it is square in most cathedrals. There is yet another rapport between half the length of the diagonal of the crossing and the diameter of the labyrinth. Are all of these relationships accidental? I think not.

Wright's proposal that the cathedral was "wrought *a priori* by means of geometry" contradicts an enormous body of work about the 12th century and Scholasticism. *A priori* means without precedent, something arrived at by deduction. Webster defines it as "made before or without examination and

27

not supported by factual study." Elaborating, Wright states, "At Chartres, function followed form." Actually, nothing could be further from the mindset in Chartres at the end of the 12th century. Emile Mâle, in *The Gothic Image: Religious Art in France of the Thirteenth Century*, states, "In medieval art, every form clothes a thought. . . . It was a vast enterprise, for all that was best in thirteenth-century thought assumed plastic form." In other words, the thought (function, purpose, meaning) came first and was then expressed in the architecture and art. Form followed function.

Sacred geometry was one of the subjects taught at the great school in Chartres. The goal of sacred geometry was to imitate the laws of God's Creation so as to most perfectly construct His home on earth. Erwin Panofsky, John W. Baldwin, Josef Pieper, and many others state that no measurement was left to chance, everything was designed to reflect a certain proportion and therefore, meaning. Far from somehow resulting from the automatic relationships formed by standard geometric shapes, the cathedral was the result of Scholasticism, the attempt to incorporate all of the knowledge from antiquity within a Christian context. It was not only highly intellectual, it followed a very well established precedent of meanings, codes, numbers, and proportions – the very opposite of *a priori*.

Chartres Cathedral: Highly intellectual and symbolic product of Scholasticism as taught in the School of Chartres.

I prefer the conclusions of John James, who believes that the most distinguished mason made the labyrinth. Such a scenario assigns the labyrinth an important place in the actual conception and design of the cathedral. For that reason, I accept 1201 as the date the labyrinth was completed. Later dates, such as the oft-used 1220, imply that the labyrinth was an afterthought, something added later. Of course I am biased, but I think the labyrinth had a greater symbolism, presence, and purpose, and so, was planned from the beginning. Perhaps, knowing that he was going to be leaving, the first mason made sure that the labyrinth was completed early on, before his departure. James points out that a temporary roof was built

28

over the nave as soon as the pillars reached the level of the capitals, and the space was used for services – another reason for installing the floor, and its labyrinth, at the earliest opportunity.

Quality of stone

The quality of the stone used to build the cathedral has also been one of the saving graces for the labyrinth. While labyrinths in some of the other cathedrals were deliberately removed because the clergy no longer appreciated them, others were destroyed when the floor had to be redone. Cathedrals were built of stone found in the immediate proximity. In the case of the cathedral in Strasbourg, for example, the stone wasn't very durable and hasn't held up very well, needing constant repair and replacement.

The floor and walls of Chartres Cathedral are made of a very dense limestone, quarried at Berchères-les-Pierres, six miles to the southeast. Almost without grain, the stone gets harder through time – despite the fact that it is rather porous. As a result of the quality of the stone, Chartres still has the original floor. I remember reading somewhere that the labyrinth and the floor had been replaced in Chartres *twice*. Not so, although it underwent minor repair in the 19th century.

Delivering the stone to the top of the hill was no small feat, especially since the route from quarry to hilltop had to cross the Eure River four times. There are several well-known mythical accounts describing so great a fervor to rebuild the cathedral that people harnessed themselves to pull the carts in order to provide the necessary stone. Today, trees and weeds have overgrown the quarry, which is barely recognizable.

Putting the labyrinth in context

One enters the nave of the cathedral, which is rectangular (four sides, symbolizing the physical plane), and proceeds toward the apse and choir in the eastern end, which is a semi-circle (the circle symbolizing the unchanging, the eternal, the divine). Hence the journey through the cathedral reflects our journey through life, from the mundane to the eternal. The same journey is expressed vertically, with the vault representing heaven. Yet, in the rectangular nave is a circular labyrinth. Even here in the midst of this world, divine perfection is found. The circle is interrupted for the entrance to the labyrinth, to allow us in. Otherwise, were the divinity unbroken, we would not find a way inside and would be left out. On the other hand, the circle is divided into four quarters, lest we forget where we are (the physical plane).

Opposite the labyrinth, in the rounded apse, the altar would have been rectangular, a bit of this world represented in the divine. (The altar has since been moved to the center of the crossing.) The cathedral is, after all, God's home on earth, not in heaven – although every effort was made to reflect heavenly splendor in the geometry, the height, the lightness, the gem-like windows. Certainly it was like entering another world. Putting a round labyrinth in the nave and a rectangular altar in the apse is not unlike a yin-yang symbol, where each element contains a dot of the opposite element, establishing an important rapport.

Upon entering the cathedral, one is surrounded by stained glass windows filled with saints and parables and the lives of Mary and Jesus. Within the hush and awe of that darkened space, we proceed from west to east, from setting sun to risen Son. First, however, we come to the labyrinth, which extends across the entire nave and can't be missed. Whereas in many cathedrals the outer doors of the western facade lead through the towers into the aisles, in Chartres, all three western doors lead directly into the nave, making it even more unlikely that someone would miss the labyrinth. Chartres has the widest nave of any of the great cathedrals in France, enabling the labyrinth to be more than 42 feet across.

Some scholars question whether the labyrinth was meant to be walked, since there are no contemporary descriptions of such activity. To that, my response is that we *do* have a written record, written in the stone and glass of the cathedral itself. It was built for use by the multitudes that couldn't read the written word, but could understand what they saw. Looking with modern eyes, the message may not be apparent to us until we learn to read the language of the architecture and the art itself. It is unmistakably there.

The labyrinth represents a mini-version of life's pilgrimage and a microcosm of the cathedral's purpose as a whole. It was taken off the wall at Lucca and out of the margins of manuscripts from Auxerre and made huge, placed on the floor where no one could avoid it. I believe it takes much more of a stretch of the imagination to conclude that people *didn't* walk it than to assume that they *did* walk it, using it for the same purpose as everything else in the cathedral, namely, the glorification of God, appreciation for Mary, and the pursuit of personal salvation. The presence of Theseus in the center further emphasized our common hero's quest to rediscover our divine nature.

Labyrinth patterns contemporary to Chartres

The labyrinth in Sens Cathedral very likely preceded the Chartres labyrinth, perhaps by several decades. The diocese of Sens included not only Chartres, but also Auxerre, where many of the earliest Chartres-like manuscript labyrinths originated. Strangely, Sens does not seem to have been a Chartres pattern. Further, there is an indication that the labyrinth in Auxerre was "of the Sens type." (No drawing of it has been found.)

Sens labyrinth as shown in book by Hermann Kern.

Two different patterns have been identified with Sens Cathedral. Hermann Kern includes a pattern with that designation in his labyrinth compendium. More recently, Craig Wright, while researching the archives in Auxerre for his book, discovered an 18th-century drawing of the Sens labyrinth prior to its destruction in 1768 when the tombstone floor was replaced with normal paving. That drawing shows a round 11-circuit labyrinth with the labryses in the same place as the Chartres pattern, but with a different path pattern, caused by entering the labyrinth in a different circuit – specifically, in the ninth circuit, like the Otfrid and Rheims patterns. Also like the Otfrid pattern, the center is very small, as it is in the classical labyrinth.

Sens labyrinth design according to drawing found by Craig Wright.

Late in the 13th century, several other cathedrals installed labyrinths, including those at Rheims and Amiens. These and several imitators in the region were all octagonal in shape, rather than round. This was likely caused by the fact that the floor was made from square tiles, which work much more easily with angular labyrinths than curved ones. Further, both the Rheims and Amiens labyrinths included figures or names of bishops and architects. It is for that reason that people sometimes speculate that the same could have been true for the missing center plaque of Chartres. We know from reliable sources, however, that it was a portrayal of Theseus and the Minotaur, not architects. In fact, architects as a separate profession didn't really exist yet when Chartres was

Rheims labyrinth, without the figures.

Rheims labyrinth made round.

built. It is only later in the 13th century that we find reports of masons who only supervise, without actually working with the stone (and getting paid more than the other masons, who grumbled somewhat).

I believe the extant 17th-century drawing of the Rheims labyrinth is not accurate. The bastions are too squashed and the lines not parallel. As a labyrinth maker, I have likely made hundreds more labyrinths than the scribes who drew a few small manuscript labyrinths centuries ago. My extensive experience gives me a certain amount of artistic license. So, in my drawing of the Rheims labyrinth, the innermost lines of the bastions align in one direction with the outermost lines of the labyrinth, while in another direction they align with the center of the labyrinth. Thus, not only are the lines parallel and much easier to draw, there is a logical rapport between the different sections of the labyrinth.

I have also drawn the Reims labyrinth round, without the bastions, just to show how the path pattern is quite different from the one at Chartres. One striking feature of the Rheims labyrinth is the size of the center, which is one-third the diameter of the labyrinth as a whole – larger even than in Chartres where the center is one-fourth the diameter. Perhaps the builders wanted to express the number three (the Trinity) rather than four.

The labryses at the top of the Rheims design are the same as in Chartres, but on the horizontal axis, on each side, the labrys on the right is moved one pathway further to the right than in the Chartres pattern. For whatever reason, the French government adopted a version of the Rheims labyrinth

32

as their official logo for historic monuments. Whether designating a church or castle or other building, the logo is a labyrinth.

The best-known octagonal labyrinth is probably the one in Amiens. Made in 1288, it has the same path pattern as the Chartres labyrinth, but made octagonal, and with a smaller center. The path and the line are of equal widths, with the path being the dark tile and the line the white tile. The distinction between path and line isn't always clear, as I have seen people in Amiens trying to walk the white path, only to discover many dead ends. They have reversed their direction and persisted, thinking it was a maze.

The original Amiens labyrinth was destroyed in 1825 and then rebuilt in 1895. The central plaque points to the cardinal directions, which are somewhat off-line with the orientation of the cathedral. One common theory has it that the cathedral is lined up with the rising sun on June 22, Saint John's Day, since the cathedral housed an important relic, the head of John the Baptist. I find that rather unlikely, since the cathedral is dedicated, like so many others, to Notre Dame, Our Lady, Mary.

Amiens labyrinth.

There was also an inscription on the Amiens labyrinth which began, "In the year of grace 1220 when the work here was initially begun, Evrart was our blessed bishop and Louis, son of Philip Augustus, king of France." It then goes on to name three architects, which it implies were in charge of the construction during the entire 68 years of building. Gothic expert John James questions whether this lineage is accurate. One part of the inscription is certainly in error, since Louis VIII didn't become King until 1222. They missed it by two years.

The Amiens labyrinth was called "House of Daedalus," thereby making

33

clear the association with the mythical Greek architect. This seems fitting given the fact that the names of the architects were included (specifically, Robert de Luzarches, Thomas de Cormont, and his son, Regnaud de Cormont). Two hundred years later, a copy of the Amiens labyrinth was installed at the Collegiate Church in nearby Saint Quentin, where it remains today, uncovered and open to the public (although it is rather beat up and there is often a bulletin board standing on it). While the labyrinth in Chartres is usually covered with chairs, the one in Amiens, like Saint Quentin, is usually accessible.

Floor in Amiens Cathdral.

A number of people have told me that they visited Chartres Cathedral and never saw the labyrinth. Perhaps the chairs hid it. Or, more likely, they were looking up at the windows rather than down at the floor. In Amiens, people often miss the labyrinth for a different reason. Then entire floor of the nave is covered with intricate geometric designs, of which the labyrinth is just one. Unless people are familiar with labyrinths, they might very well overlook it as just another decoration.

When I make octagonal labyrinths, I don't use Amiens as my model, as I find the wide lines take up too much space. Instead, I use a design more like the octagonal labyrinth in Sélestat, in Alsace. Built at the church of Saint Foy in the 19th century, it has path/line ratios similar to the Chartres labyrinth. I drew such a design recently, for an octagonal Chartres-style labyrinth made of vinyl tile squares. The paths were 12 inches wide, allowing for whole, uncut tiles, whereas the lines were 2½ inches wide. Essentially, the pattern was comprised of two square grids, turned at 45-degree angles to each other. The line pieces and 45-degree angle cuts can all be made in advance, and then the labyrinth assembled. In a circular labyrinth, each line has a different radius, which makes things much more complicated.

The Chartres path pattern

Another labyrinth contemporary with Chartres existed in the cathedral in Poitiers. The labyrinth is gone, but a graffito remains which someone

34

scratched onto the wall. It has one place in which the line leading into the center was extended so that it touches another line, thereby creating an intersection. Perhaps the artist was deliberately seeking symmetry for the tree-like figure.

What has been drawn in the graffito is not the lines of the labyrinth but the pattern of the path itself – the pattern actually walked. For comparison, I have included a more accurate drawing of the route one walks on the Chartres labyrinth. Hermann Kern calls this kind of path mapping "Ariadne's thread."

Graffito in Poitiers based on the original labyrinth.

We can learn quite a bit about the nature of the Chartres labyrinth by examining its path. For instance, the path pattern is a reflection of itself. Although the size of the circles differs, note that the pattern entering the labyrinth (straight, detour, straight, half circle to the left, half circle to the left, quarter circle to the right, quarter circle to the left, etc.) is the same as the pattern exiting from the center of the labyrinth. In fact, the two reflections "meet" at the top of the labyrinth in the sixth circuit.

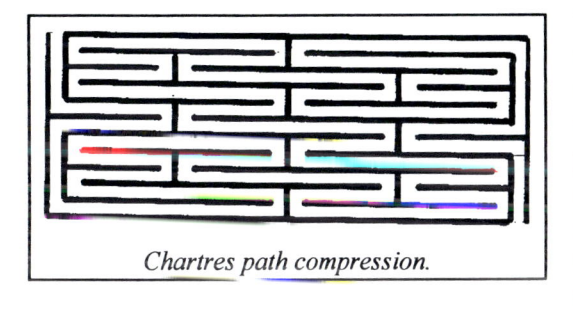

Chartres path pattern.

Chartres path compression.

There are a number of ways of showing the symmetry and rhythm of the path pattern. One is to use a compression drawing. In this illustration, the center of the labyrinth is at the top and the perimeter at the

35

bottom. The labryses show as vertical lines, dividing the pattern into quadrants, just as in the circular version. The first time I saw this compression drawing, I was very impressed by the regularity of what, at first glace, seems so complicated.

As we can see, the path pattern is actually very well organized. Another way to show this is to plot the progress through the various quadrants of the labyrinth. The lower left quadrant, in which the entrance is located, is quadrant number one. Going around the labyrinth clockwise, the upper left quadrant is number two, upper right number three, and lower right number four. The lines in the graph to the left indicate paths that span from one quadrant to another. If you turned this graph upside down, it would be the same. Is such elegant symmetry automatic or planned? Does it come naturally with the geometry or must it be choreographed? For comparison, let's look at diagrams for four different labyrinths.

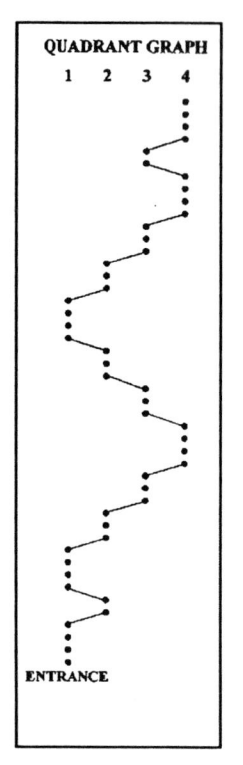

The four graphs on the next page illustrate which circuit the path passes through. In other words, they show in what order the 11 circuits are walked, according to the number of the circuit. The circuits are numbered 1-11 from the inside (top of graph) outward. The numbers zero and 12 represent the center and the entrance, respectively. Each column represents one segment of the path between turns.

As you can see at a glance, the Chartres labyrinth is quite different. Immediately upon entering, it takes you directly to the first circuit, right next to the center, as if to show you the goal. It then works its way further out. When you feel like you are the furthest away, suddenly, *voila*, you go right to the center. The other three labyrinths begin at the perimeter and slowly work their way towards the center. In the Chartres and Rheims patterns, the straight paths are encountered only at the beginning and end of the walk, when entering the labyrinth and when entering the center. In the two Sens versions, however, some portions of the straight paths are walked midway through the labyrinth. The Kern Sens version is the only one that is not symmetrical. It seems to me that anyone can figure out a path that reaches the center. To do it with balance and elegance, however, is another matter entirely.

36

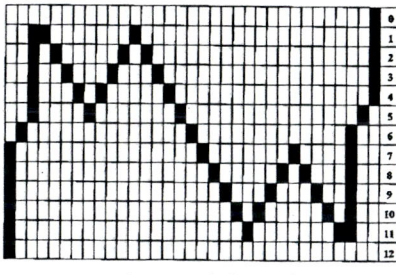

Chartres labyrinth.

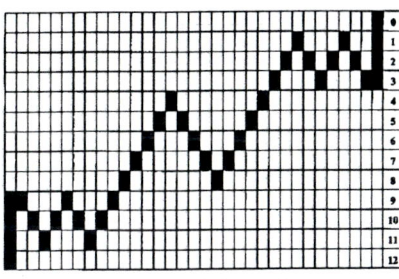

Rheims labyrinth.

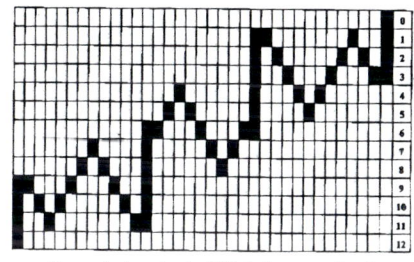

Sens labyrinth (Wright version).

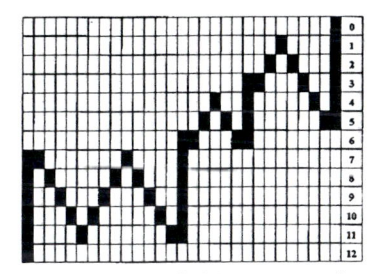

Sens labyrinth (Kern version).

The path through the Chartres labyrinth has another unique aspect with regards to the order in which certain areas of the labyrinth are walked. It first takes the walker to the inside of the labyrinth on the left side, then to the inside on the right, then to the outside left and finally, the outside right. Other labyrinth designs wander around without this cohesive progression. The same Chartres path pattern illustrated on page 35 (Ariadne's thread) is shown to the left, this time with each area walked given a different pattern. It clearly shows how carefully grouped the paths are.

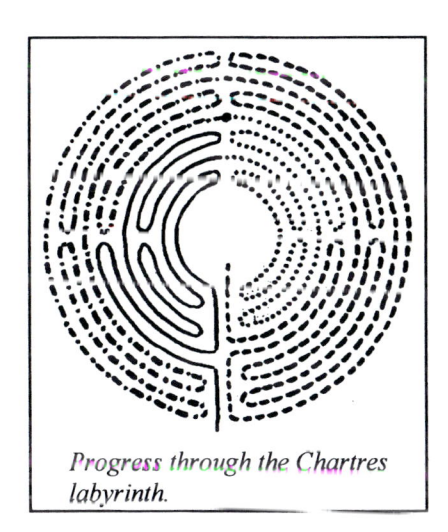

Progress through the Chartres labyrinth.

During my many visits to Chartres (46 as of this writing), I became good friends with the rector (now retired) of the cathedral, François Legaux. In fact, during one tour to France that I led for the Rev. Dr. Lauren Artress, canon at Grace Cathedral in San Francisco, I introduced Dr. Artress and Father Legaux, which proved

37

Inside left.

Inside right.

Outside left.

Outside right.

to be the beginning of a long and fruitful relationship between their two cathedrals.

On one occasion, Father Legaux showed me a series of black-and-white photographs taken from the organ loft, showing a group of people walking in procession through the labyrinth. The entire group of photos will be included in a full-length book I am currently writing. The four included here show the four stages of progress through the labyrinth described above.

When entering the labyrinth, it is always on an odd-numbered circuit. Counting from the center outward, it is circuit number seven in the Chartres labyrinth and circuit number nine in the Rheims and Sens labyrinths. From that circuit, whether turning left or right into the adjacent circuits, the walker changes direction. As a result, in the even-numbered circuits he will always be going counter-clockwise. Turning either left or right from an even-numbered circuit will take the walker back in a clockwise direction, on an odd-numbered circuit.

Knowing this fact, one can look at anyone walking the labyrinth and tell whether they are on their way in or out.

When they are on an odd-numbered circuit, simply note whether they are going clockwise (heading inward) or counter-clockwise (heading back out).

It sometimes happens that people walking into the labyrinth never reach the center. Instead, they find themselves back at the entrance. Similarly, people exiting from the center sometimes find themselves back at the center. What went wrong? This would not happen by walking over a labrys and staying in the same circuit, as their direction on that circuit (clockwise or counter-clockwise) would remain the same. It can happen only by swerving into an adjacent path without changing direction. So doing, one changes from entering to exiting, or vice versa.

Energies in the labyrinth

There are many people who have dowsed or otherwise measured the energy within the labyrinth in Chartres (and other sacred places). Dowsers are most often associated with using forked sticks to locate water. There is much more to dowsing than that, however. Dowsing is a method for tapping into the great Wisdom that is available to all of us when we are attuned to it. Dowsing instruments can be used to answer yes-or-no questions, to determine plans of action, and to locate energies as well as water.

In March of 2001 I was visiting Chartres when I came across a friend there, Willem Kuipers from Holland. We had met the previous year at a labyrinth conference. He had two "L" rods with him, which are used for dowsing. Holding one rod in each hand and keeping them parallel to the pavement, he proposed to walk the labyrinth and note how the rods changed direction, to see if there was any pattern or direction to the flow of the energy.

We spent the next hour walking the labyrinth together, he with the "L" rods and I with a pen and clipboard, stopping every few feet to make arrows on a paper labyrinth in the direction indicated by the dowsing rods. The results were irregular, without any seeming pattern. That's not to say there isn't a pattern to the energy, only that our particular effort was not successful. On a broader scale, dowsers and others at sacred sites have located the presence of water domes, energy lines, places where energy is either high or low, and much more.

The first time I ever walked a labyrinth was at Chartres on the morning of the summer solstice in June, 1995. I was the fourth person in line just after the cathedral opened. Ahead of me were my wife and a couple from Holland. The man, who was the first to enter the labyrinth, was dowsing with a pendulum as he walked. It was a small object on a chain that would swing in various ways. I noticed that just as he made the final turn and headed towards the entrance into the center of the labyrinth, the pendulum was very active, making wide and rapid circles, apparently indicating a high degree of energy.

I have not pursued a study of the labyrinth from the point of view of energy, and so no additional considerations are included here. It is not clear to me whether sacred sites are built where there is lots of energy, or whether the energy accumulates *after* the site has been built, by the great amount of devotion and prayer expressed there. When constructing labyrinths, dowsers use their skills to ask the earth where the labyrinth should be, what size it is, what direction it faces, and so forth. More information on this topic is available at Sig Lonegren's website at www.geomancy.org.

I am frequently asked about the prescribed orientation of a labyrinth. My response is always, "that depends." The nature of the site itself may determine the best location for the entrance to face. Or one can use dowsing or some other intuitive method of feeling into the best decision. Sometimes I just spend time on the site of the labyrinth until a certain direction seems obvious to me. However, with regards to church labyrinths, a completely different parameter applies. Church labyrinths were almost all built with the entrances facing the western doors of the cathedral, so that when you walk into the cathedral, you find yourself at the entrance to the labyrinth. To utilize that symbolism, dowsing is not be required. Simply face the labyrinth towards the west. Alternatively, if the church itself faces a different direction, align the labyrinth with the church.

Later developments based on the Chartres pattern

While the Chartres labyrinth has been widely copied, sometimes the designs have incorporated certain changes and variations. In the 16th century, in Toulouse and Mirepoix, labyrinths were made as decorations on nine ceramic tiles. In the latter case, the design is right-handed. Perhaps that was the result of having traced the one in Toulouse, which was left-handed. Or perhaps it was based on the example in the notebook of Villard de Honnecourt, who drew a right-handed labyrinth. What is somewhat unusual for a labyrinth of such late date is the fact that in Mirepoix, a devil-like figure was placed in the center, reminiscent of the Minotaurs placed in 12th- and 13th-century labyrinths. A similar 16th-century tile labyrinth was reported in Pont-l'Abbé in Brittany, but no drawings or other proof have been found.

One of the more interesting variations of the Chartres pattern was constructed in the monastery church of Saint Bertin in Saint Omer, in northern France. It is made of black and white tiles in a grid of 49 tiles square. This is a significant number, as it represents the square of the mystical number seven (7 x 7 = 49). Kern failed to see the relationship between this design and that of Chartres. However, I felt it must exist due to the fact that it has 11 circuits and that the order in which the labyrinth is walked – inner left, inner right, outer left, outer right – is a pattern we can now attribute to the Chartres labyrinth.

The Chartres pattern on a 49-square grid.

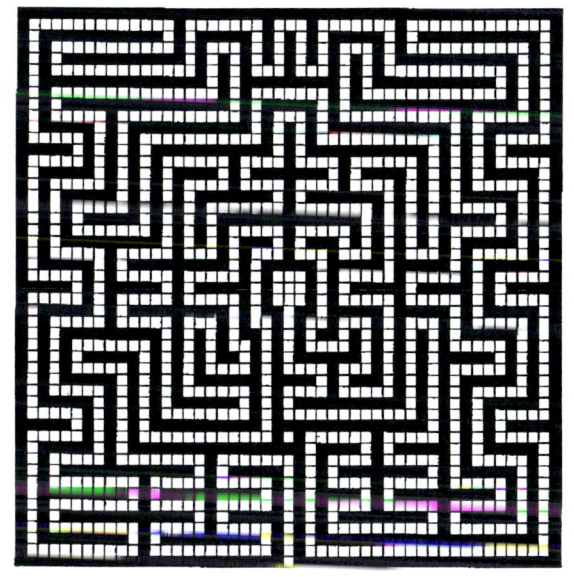

Given my attention, the Saint Omer labyrinth soon revealed other parallels. To see them, I first made a Chartres pattern on a similar 49-tile square grid. It required that the center be smaller than usual. Next, I used felt-tipped pens of seven different colors, marking the various sections of the path through the square Chartres labyrinth. For the first section I started at the entrance, went through

The Saint Omer design.

41

the detour, and ended up on the first circuit next to the center. Using the same color on the Saint Omer pattern, I was able to enter, go through a more complicated detour, and still end up next to the center. The next segment in the Chartres pattern comprised the two half circles in circuits one and two, followed by two quarter circles and another half circle. In the Saint Omer pattern, I was able to do the same thing. Eventually, I was able to find the matching paths through each of the labyrinths, showing the derivation of one from the other. Using the two illustrations on page 41, you can discover the similarities for yourself.

Another Chartres-like labyrinth worth mentioning was discovered in 1954 in a small church in Genainville, not far from Mantes-la-Jolie. It was engraved onto a stone which was unearthed during some renovations. Small and rather damaged, the pattern is interesting because it is octagonal with four bastions. It resembles the labyrinth in Rheims, which also had four bastions. But the Rheims pattern was *different* from the Chartres pattern, whereas in Genainville the labyrinth *follows* the Chartres path pattern – although right-handed. Unlike Rheims, one does not enter into the bastions while walking the labyrinth, although that could be accomplished very easily. This might be a nice Chartres design for a space in which the labyrinth needs to be square rather than round.

Genainville labyrinth.

Modern Chartres variations

For a decade now, the labyrinth has been gaining popularity as a spiritual tool. Because the Chartres labyrinth design has specific Christian origins, it is usually the one chosen by churches. The labyrinth revival has been led by the Rev. Dr. Lauren Artress at Grace Cathedral in San Francisco. The portable canvas labyrinths sold through Veriditas, the labyrinth organization founded by Artress at Grace Cathedral, are actually variations on the original pattern. First, the labryses are much wider. To balance them, the space between the petals is also painted in, giving more weight to the center.

The purpose for the larger labryses is to allow someone to step off the path and get out of the way of "traffic." This variation is particularly suited for

"Pure" Chartres labyrinth.

Veriditas variation.

the meditative use of the labyrinth. Since we at the Labyrinth Enterprises make the Chartres canvas labyrinths sold through Grace Cathedral, we are familiar with this variation, which is quite popular.

The Rev. Dr. Lauren Artress discovered the Chartres labyrinth at a mystery school run by Jean Houston. Artress returned to Grace Cathedral where she engaged the services of Richard Feather Anderson to help make a portable canvas labyrinth. As she began traveling with the labyrinth, introducing it as a tool for prayer and well-being, churches she visited asked where they might also obtain a labyrinth.

The "real thing," the labyrinth in Chartres surrounded by candles.

Canvas labyrinth by Labyrinth Enterprises.

It was that need which led me to become a labyrinth maker. During the past five years, I have produced more than 650 portable labyrinths, most of them with the Chartres design or some variation. I have also written a number of instruction manuals (listed on our website) for those who wish to make their own labyrinths. In fact, our website has considerable useful information about labyrinths.

43

"Petite Chartres" 7-circuit pattern on canvas.

Canvas "Heart of Chartres" 5-circuit design.

Chartres labyrinth made of stones and rubber "mulch."

Outdoor acrylic Chartres labyrinth on concrete pebble aggregate terrace.

For churches without enough room for the full Chartres pattern, smaller versions have evolved. Of course they aren't really Chartres patterns. One can only say that they resemble the labyrinth in Chartres. The two examples shown above were designed by the author and are part of the product line of Labyrinth Enterprises. The "Petite Chartres" is 24 feet in diameter, while the "Heart of Chartres" is 12 feet across.

The original Chartres labyrinth was indoors, made of three-inch-thick limestone and marble, carved and inlaid into the floor. Now, during the modern labyrinth revival, Chartres labyrinths are being made outdoors as often as indoors, from materials as diverse as acrylic resin, concrete, stones and mulch, bricks and pavers, and more. Temporary labyrinths are being made from masking tape, by painting the grass, laying out wooden blocks or rope, and even by sticking turkey feathers, plastic forks or brightly colored wire engineers' flags into

The author making a demonstration Chartres labyrinth from masking tape.

Details of masking tape Chartres labyrinth 104 feet in diameter walked by 2000 people on New Year's Eve, 1998 (and removed the next day). It took 13 people three hours to make the labyrinth.

the ground. The Chartres labyrinth pattern has existed for more than a thousand years. Now, perhaps more than ever in its history, it is being appreciated and used. Inevitably, this leads to new applications, variations, and construction techniques.

Tradition

While I am far from being a purist, I do favor good workmanship and tradition. By using traditional labyrinth patterns, we can join the many thousands – probably millions – who have gone before us in walking the same pattern. The master of Chartres looked to the past and included long-established symbolism and ancient knowledge in the cathedral and the labyrinth, following the lead of what had come before, thereby connecting with it.

In modern times, there is a strong tendency in the other direction, to make something unique and to put our names on it, proudly claiming that we have done something no one else has ever done. Personally, I never sign my Chartres labyrinths. If anonymity was good enough for the great master of Chartres, I figure it is good enough for me. Of course, having made a number of Chartres derivatives, I have clearly gone in non-traditional directions as well.

Whoever that unknown master was who laid out the cathedral and made the labyrinth in Chartres, we salute you. I recall the time I was standing in the nave of Chartres Cathedral when a couple came in the front entrance, along with their young son. The child blinked for a moment to adjust his eyes to the darkness, and then looked up, exclaiming in a loud voice, "Wow-w-w-w-w-w-w-w-w!" If the master of Chartres was looking down from his deserved mansion in Heaven, I suspect he smiled and said, "He got it." I hope that we, too, can "get" it by appreciating the Chartres labyrinth, its setting and history, its elegant design and symbolism, and most of all by using it – thereby availing ourselves of this powerful and universal spiritual tool that can lead us not only to its center, but to ourselves and to God.

Contact us

We welcome your comments and suggestions about any of our publications and materials. Our publications can be ordered at the address below.

>Labyrinth Enterprises
>128 Slocum Avenue
>St. Louis, MO 63119
>
>Tel: (314) 968-5557 or (800) 873-9873
>Fax: (314) 968-5539 or (888) 873-9873
>
>Web: www.labyrinth-enterprises.com
>Email: robert@labyrinth-enterprises.com

PUBLICATIONS FROM LABYRINTH ENTERPRISES
128 Slocum Avenue, St. Louis, MO 63119
www.labyrinth-enterprises.com • (800) 873-9873

The Labyrinth Revival
This is a beginning primer on labyrinths, suitable for giving to someone who knows little about the subject. It touches briefly on a variety of topics outlining where labyrinths come from and how they may be used. $10

Constructing the Chartres Labyrinth
This detailed, step-by-step manual covers all of the instructions for making a Chartres labyrinth, including specialized tools, patterns, proportions, and many little tips and secrets. $20

Origin, Symbolism, and Design of the Chartres Labyrinth
This book is for those who want to learn more about the Chartres labyrinth. It originated over a period of several centuries, as illustrations in manuscripts. The most elegant of labyrinth designs, it incorporates much sacred geometry and symbolism. $10

Constructing Classical Labyrinths
This detailed, step-by-step manual covers various methods for making classical labyrinths with a variety of materials. $20

Church Labyrinths
Questions and answers regarding the history, relevance, and use of labyrinths in churches. Written in language acceptable to any church board of directors.
$10

Accurate drawings of the Chartres Labyrinth
8½ by 11 inches $2
18 inches, laminated (could be used as finger labyrinth) $10
Computer Aided Drafting (CAD) $50

Postage and handling
Books = $2.50 for the first item, $1.25 each additional
Drawings   8½-inch = $2.00   18-inch = $3.50
CAD = No charge

Wholesale discounts available on some items.